P9-BZD-860

# I Can If I Want To

# I Can If I Want To

*Arnold Lazarus, Ph.D.*
*and Allen Fay, M.D.*

William Morrow and Company, Inc., New York 1975

Printed in the United States of America.

1 2 3 4 5 79 78 77 76 75

**Library of Congress Cataloging in Publication Data**

Lazarus, Arnold A
I can if I want to.

1. Success. 2. Rational-emotive psychotherapy.
I. Fay, Allen, joint author. II. Title.
BF637.S8L38 158'.1 75-11744
ISBN 0-688-02941-8

*Book design: Helen Roberts*

# Contents

# I Can If I Want To

# Who We Are and How This Book Came to Be

This book is the outcome of a personal and professional association dating back to the fall of 1972, when the authors met at a workshop conducted by one of us, Arnold Lazarus. It represents the collaborative effort of a professor of psychology (A.L.), whose major activity is the training and supervising of therapists while also conducting a part-time therapy practice, and a psychiatrist, Allen Fay, who is in full-time practice but who teaches residents and medical students on a part-time basis.

Over the past three years we have shared many experiences. While conducting our respective private practices, we have sat in on each other's groups and individual sessions, served as co-therapists, conducted workshops and seminars, and exchanged information on a variety of topics. It became evident that although our training and backgrounds were very different, we had evolved similar therapeutic styles, adopted similar methods and techniques, and developed an almost identical outlook and philosophy of life. We spent literally hundreds of hours discussing our frustrations about the limitations of the art and science of therapy and our disenchantment with factionalism, each school of psychology claiming to have the answer, the correct approach.

As we observed each other at work, discussed our failures and successes, conferred about difficult cases, and disclosed our own hang-ups, we realized that people with very different problems seemed to be making the same basic mistakes over and over again. This led us to test a variety of different methods for overcoming in a short time the common mistakes that produce so much unhappiness. Our conclusions have led us to write this book.

# What We've Learned About People and How We're Planning to Help You Change

Why are we consulted by so many hardworking, successful, productive people who have "made it" but who nevertheless feel anxious, miserable, empty, and inwardly unfulfilled? They were told to "get ahead," to "win and compete," to "play it cool," to "perform and achieve." And they did. Furthermore, they kept up appearances, they learned how to impress people, how to please others, how to hide their faults, and how to keep their inner thoughts and needs to themselves. They worked hard and excelled. They tried to keep up with the latest. They tended to strive for perfection. They watched their language and their manners. They were never idle. But none of them seemed to find happiness. Instead, they were often anxious, compulsive, or simply miserable. They often suffered from ulcers, tension headaches, or insomnia.

## *Something Is Wrong!*

An eminent surgeon, widely respected and admired, confides that he finds life meaningless. He comes from the "right" family. He has worked hard at the "right" schools, in the "right" hospitals, and has achieved fame, fortune, and recognition. Yet he finds life meaningless!

Another man believes that he is unhappy because he has not achieved fame or fortune. He did not attend the "right" schools or meet the "right" contacts. If only he had "made it" he would be happy.

A forty-year-old woman who had won two national beauty contests nearly twenty years ago has been feeling more and more depressed over the past ten years. She has never learned to attach much value to anything but external appearances, and now that her youthful looks are fading she agonizes and has nothing with which to replace them.

We acquire our values, beliefs, and attitudes from the people with whom we associate—especially from parents, teachers and peers—from the mass media, and from a variety of other experiences. If we try to follow the guides to successful, happy living as laid down by our society, many of us will end up with unsuccessful, miserable existences. *The theme of this book is that although well-meaning others have duped us (and themselves) into believing a mass of fallacies about how to lead satisfying and worthwhile lives we can nevertheless free ourselves from these absurd and destructive notions.*

These faulty values make us uptight, afraid of criticism and rejection, overanxious about approval and disapproval, prone to feelings of guilt, and obsessed with polar opposites such as "succeeding" or "failing." These fallacies interfere with every aspect of our lives. They mar sexual fulfillment, undermine the relationship between husband and wife, parent and child, employer and employee, and they destroy the potential for true friendship.

Nearly everyone with whom we have ever discussed these misconceptions seems to be aware of them. They all pay lip service to the negative effects of overcompetitive strivings, extreme levels of ambition, people-pleasing, and phony facades. Our patients or clients tell us that they already know about these pitfalls. Yet they continue to display the very same pernicious behaviors in all walks of life. We have never met a person, no matter how humanistic, seemingly rational, and nonmaterialistic who does not commit some of these common mistakes and whose life is not less livable because of it! But being aware of the various mistakes that create havoc is insufficient. We have to *do* something about them. Straightforward, deliberate, and systematic rethinking is the first step toward a constructive change in our feelings and emotions. But even rethinking is not enough. In addition, we have to act differently, we have to *change our behaviors* if we really wish to change our lives.

This book can change your life! We mean it, and we shall show you how to go about it. We will point out to you:

1. Basic mistakes that ruin your life.
2. Faulty assumptions behind these mistakes.
3. The twofold way in which you'll combat the mistakes:
   *a.* By changing your thinking.
   *b.* By changing your behavior.

You do not have to wade through hundreds of words to extract the basic messages. They are outlined in easy-to-read, step-by-step form. Don't feel insulted by the simplicity and repetition; scientific studies have shown that these are two essential elements in learning and psychological change.

When you read through the various mistakes and the faulty reasoning that accompanies them, you will almost surely recognize some of your own misconceptions. We recommend concentrating on the errors that are most applicable to you and following the strategies that are specifically designed to eliminate them. This book covers the most *common mistakes* we have observed in our patients, colleagues, friends, acquaintances, and in ourselves. You may note some overlap between mistakes, but each mistake, we feel, possesses distinctive features meriting separate treatment.

We have drawn our ideas from many sources, including, of course, our own clinical experience. We hope that the way in which the ideas and strategies are presented will be sufficiently different and compelling to set this "how-to" manual apart from the run-of-the-mill self-help publications. We cannot acknowledge everyone from whom we have borrowed ideas, but we have been profoundly influenced by Albert Bandura, Albert Ellis, Jay Haley, Sidney Jourard, O. H. Mowrer,

*Arnold Lazarus/Allen Fay*

and Andrew Salter. Special thanks are due the many people who have consulted us—from them we have learned the most.

# Getting Started

Human beings, unlike any other species on earth, have the unique capacity for instant change. People are capable of making immediate and long-lasting decisions that can have a profound influence on their emotional well-being. In other words, even if someone has responded incorrectly or "neurotically" to a given situation for many years on end, a systematic corrective exercise can often undo the problem there and then. We have seen this happen dozens of times.

For example, a woman had suffered from anxiety attacks for many years. She had seen several psychiatrists, a hypnotist, and a few psychologists over the years, but her anxiety continued to limit her range of activities. We suggested the following procedure to her: "Talk to your anxiety as if it were a naughty child. You can say, 'Now you stop that this moment!' 'Now you start behaving yourself!' 'I said Stop!' Just keep on reprimanding the anxiety in this manner. Many people find that this causes the anxiety to weaken and disappear." Indeed, the woman tested the "Stop!" technique for herself and found, to her amazement, that she could keep her anxiety in check. Little by little she gained self-confidence and soon overcame her debilitating fears entirely. Thus, a simple technique enabled her to change her life.

You may think the foregoing is preposterous. How can such a simple-minded technique prove so effective? Surely human problems are far too complex for anything so simplistic to have far-reaching effects. Isn't it true that emotional difficulties call for time-consuming and involved procedures in order to understand and fully overcome them? NO! These mistaken beliefs cause many people to give up hope about changing their lives and solving their emotional problems.

The most widespread myths about change are the following:

Myth #1: If you have knowledge and understanding—in other words, if you know why you are the way you are, or why you do the things you do, or why you feel the way you feel—then you will change.

Myth #2: If you don't know the reasons behind your behavior, you won't change.

Myth #3: It takes a long time to change. After all, you have had problems for a long time.

Myth #4: If you change fairly quickly, it is superficial and it won't last.

Myth #5: It is frequently impossible to change. "This is the way I am, and this is the way I'll always be."

Myth #6: If you are middle-aged or older, it is too late to change.

THESE COMMON BELIEFS ARE ABSOLUTELY FALSE AND LEAD MANY PEOPLE TO DOUBT THEIR CAPACITY TO CHANGE.

Now what are we claiming? That all or nearly all cases of anxiety will respond to the "Stop!" technique? That the majority of complex problems can be resolved by one simple procedure? No. We recognize that there is often no substitute for the systematic retraining of faulty attitudes, self-defeating behaviors, and negative feelings. Nevertheless, an important point needs to be emphasized: We have seen numerous people with long-standing and seemingly intricate problems *who dramatically changed their lives the moment they started applying the principles and procedures outlined in this book*. In other words, as soon as a person makes the decision to embark on a corrective course of action—keeping notes as we recommend, taking prescribed risks, and carrying out the other assignments described herein—this already constitutes a change that can have remarkable benefits.

Why should *you* be different from these people? You're not, and as you read this book you will be able to identify your own faulty behaviors and mistaken attitudes. Then, by applying the corrective exercises we provide here, you will note definite improvements in self-esteem and confidence. We estimate that in *one day*, you will be able to read this book, recognize your own "neurotic" errors, start keeping notes, try out some new behaviors, do some rethinking, and thus begin to feel a definite change in your life for the better. Once you get started on an established path of corrective thinking and constructive behavior, you will make more and more profound and satisfying changes hour by hour and day by day. That is why we have called this book *I Can If I Want To.*

## Therapy as Education

We view therapy as education. It took us a long time to discover how simple it can be to change a lifetime pattern of suffering and anguish. We had to unlearn many of the attitudes and theories we had learned in our training and in our own therapy. For example, we had to realize that people with problems are not defective, that emotional hangups—even severe ones—are not illnesses, that we are not victims of deep-seated unconscious forces, and that therapists are not superior to the people who consult them. When one has been thoroughly trained to regard bad habits as diseases, to search for hidden meanings, to read great significance into passing utterances, to diagnose and label people and their problems, it is difficult to recognize one of the most profound truths of all—*psychological change calls for problem solving in the here and now rather than preoccupation with the hereafter or the heretofore.*

One of us, looking a little green on the first day of clinical training, was counseled by a more advanced student to follow two guidelines in order to stay out of trouble: "Don't answer any of the patients' questions, and don't say anything about yourself." This was the worst possible advice. Emotional problems are learned.

People *learn* to think, feel, and behave the way they do, and they can *unlearn* the unproductive (neurotic) patterns they have acquired. One of the most fundamental ways in which learning occurs is through observation and the sharing of experiences. Thus, the therapist who talks very little and who discloses hardly anything about him(her)self deprives the patient or client of a vital learning experience essential for change.

*We firmly believe that therapy is education rather than healing; that it is growth rather than treatment.*

Once people realize that overcoming emotional problems is an educational process, the concept of *self-education* is easily understood. In the same way as it is possible to teach oneself gourmet cooking, a foreign language, or how to type, psychological self-help is entirely feasible. In fact in the professional literature of late, there has been an enormous amount of data confirming the value of self-management and self-help procedures.

## Unhappiness Is Self-created

The tendency to attribute unhappiness to external sources is widespread. It is one of the most serious psychological mistakes. People say: "His remark upset me!" "Her comments hurt me!" "It made me unhappy when he left the room." In reality, remarks, comments and statements do not hurt or upset people. *They upset themselves over these statements or incidents.* The age-old saying (like most age-old sayings) remains profoundly true: "Sticks and stones may break my bones but words can never hurt me!" Though we utter these ideas as children, we do not take them seriously as adults. If we did, we would then say: "I upset myself over his remark," in place of the psychologically inaccurate version, "His remark upset me!" Similarly, we would say: "I hurt myself over her comments," "I made myself unhappy when he left the room," "I distressed myself over the fact that he ignored me."

As long as we incorrectly blame outside sources for our miseries, it remains impossible to do much about them. However, if we realize that *we upset ourselves* over the things that happen to us, we can work at changing. The first step is to ask: "Exactly how do I manage to upset myself?" We then obtain the clues about how to avoid upsetting ourselves.

For example, a young man was extremely distressed because his girl friend refused to stop dating other men. "Her behavior really upsets me," he said. "No," we replied, "you are upsetting yourself over her behavior." And then we asked: "How are you managing to upset yourself so deeply? What are you saying to yourself?" It took about 10 minutes to piece together the fact that he was upsetting himself by thinking along the following lines: "I am failing as a man. If I were any good, she would want to go out with me exclusively. There must be a serious deficiency in me. She probably finds other men better-looking, more virile, more interesting, and more stimulating. I'll probably never find anyone who will regard me as really worthwhile." Once we knew how he was so successfully upsetting himself we were in a position to show him how to stop making himself so unhappy over his present girl friend's lack of ardor. We told him to challenge each one of his negative self-statements. "How does failure with one woman [or even ten women] add up to being a failure *as a man?* It means that a relationship didn't work out as you had hoped. It says nothing about you as a man in general. How do you know that there is not some quirk in her that prevents her from developing the degree of attachment you would desire?"

The point is that when we recognize where the locus of control resides—*in our heads and not in the external events*—we are able to start doing something to change the way we perceive events. If you make yourself unhappy when your spouse yells at you, or when your in-laws visit you, or when your neighbor's dog barks, you must first discover exactly how you go about inducing this unhappiness. Then you can decide to do something about it.

## How to Change

We are now going to show you how to bring about change by demonstrating the specific approach set forth in this book. Remember: people wrongly blame external factors for their moods and behaviors! How often have *you* said something like: "He made me angry." "She ruined my day." "Those kids are going to give me a heart attack." "My sister-in-law infuriates me." "His attitude upset me." Our guess is that you, like almost everyone, often attribute your feelings and reactions to external events. We simply have not been taught to say: "I made myself angry over his remark."

"I allowed her behavior to get in the way of my own pleasure." Few people realize that by talking and thinking in this accurate manner, they immediately create ways of controlling negative situations. Thus, the person who says, "I upset myself over the fact that my wife came home late," instead of the usual "My wife upset me by coming home late," can ask how he went about upsetting himself. Then he would be able to learn how to stop upsetting himself in the future.

The basic tenet of one school of psychotherapy—rational emotive therapy—is the age-old observation that we are not disturbed by things—external events—but by the views we take of them—our own perceptions. Much of our thinking derives from this school and we strongly subscribe to their basic tenets. If you accept this philosophy—and it is our aim to convince you it is correct—and wish to change your own reactions, here is what you would need to do:

1. *Talk to your friends about the relationship between external events and people's reactions to those events.* A good way to learn something yourself is to teach others. As you explain to others how we miss the point when we say things like, "The way she put me down depressed me," instead of "I made myself feel depressed over the way she put me down," you will be educating them while helping yourself.

2. *Whenever you catch yourself falsely attributing your own feelings to external events, keep a record of this in a notebook, making a notation as soon as it is possible.* This is going to become an important factor in your growth and change. A typical page in your notebook might look something like this:

| | | |
|---|---|---|
| Tuesday | 11:30 A.M. | Blamed my depression on the boss's temper. |
| | 3:15 P.M. | Accused Tom of hurting my feelings. |
| | 10:20 P.M. | Told Sally that her mother makes me uptight. |
| Wednesday | 9:10 A.M. | I said the boss is going to drive me to drink. |
| | Midnight | Told Sally I couldn't sleep because she had upset me. |
| Thursday | 3 P.M. | Told Mildred that Tom ruined my morning. |
| Friday | 6 P.M. | Said I was depressed because the party was canceled. |
| Sunday | 4:45 P.M. | Said I'm in a bad mood because my team lost the game. |

3. *Set aside a definite time to correct the faulty reasoning.* Thus, during lunch hour on Wednesday, the three entries made on Tuesday could be thought through.

*a.* "The boss's temper can't depress me. I depress myself over his temper. How do I go about doing that? Well, when he yells and carries on, I think to myself that he might fire me. So I guess it's not his temper that depresses me, but I make myself miserable by thinking that he might fire me. Perhaps I could stop worrying so much about being fired."

*b.* "Tom can't hurt my feelings. I let my feelings get hurt by the fact that he invited Debbie to lunch in front of me. I told myself that this means he dislikes me. Actually I think he prefers Debbie's company to mine. That makes sense because they both go in for boats and water skiing and other things that turn me off. Why let my feelings get hurt by that?"

*c.* "How do I make myself uptight over Sally's mother? I guess I would like her to approve of me and I make myself upset when she is critical. Actually, why do I want her approval? She's an old-fashioned woman with ideas that just don't jibe with mine. So if I take her for what she is, I don't think she will get to me again."

Note what we are doing here: we are recommending an active process, the systematic use of applied psychology. We are not talking theoretically and abstractly. Throughout the book you will be asked to *do* specific things. You will be shown how to identify specific responses you wish to change, how to monitor faulty thoughts, feelings and behaviors, and how to introduce new and corrective responses into your repertoire. Many people waste inordinate amounts of time struggling to change by exploring the deeper recesses of the mind, by delving into their early life, by analyzing their dreams, by reading ponderous tomes, and through philosophical reflections about the meaning of life. Life is too short and that struggle too long.

## *Why Many People Don't Change*

In the foregoing pages, you have come across several notions and suggestions that you may have found provocative or stimulating. Frequently, we read something and nod in recognition of basic truths or react with interest to a new insight. Unfortunately, despite the recognition and the knowledge, many who read self-help books or even undergo extensive therapy do not change.

Rapid long-lasting and meaningful improvements in psychological functioning call for at least two specific areas of intervention: (1) we need to correct irrational thinking; *and* (2) we need to overcome negative behaviors. We firmly believe that you can achieve these ends by applying the basic principles we are outlining here.

Why do so many people fail to derive help or to change even after years of therapy? The failure, we feel, results from:

1. Misconceptions about the nature and intention of therapy. Many people believe that the purpose of therapy is to talk about their problems, rather than devising active means of solving these problems. *It is not talk that is important, but action.*

2. Poor chemistry between patient and therapist.

3. The absence of several conditions that we feel are essential for change to occur.

What are these essential conditions?

*a. Identifying something as a problem.* There are many people who seem to be unfulfilled and seem to suffer, but who do not see themselves as having problems.

*b. Accepting the possibility that something can be done about it.* There are many people who say they have problems but who feel that that's the way they are and nothing can be done about it.

*c. Expressing a desire to change.* Again, there are many people who say that they have problems and who acknowledge the possibility of change but who seem uninterested in changing.

*d. A willingness to work and to make an effort to change.* This is *crucial* in distinguishing people who change from those who don't. If people are willing to work at changing their thinking and behaving, which includes keeping notebooks and practicing the techniques that are outlined in this book, the likelihood of change becomes much greater. We have found a startling difference among people who come for therapy. Those who keep notes, draw up charts, and read the books that are recommended, consistently change in a constructive direction. The fact is that psychological growth and emotional re-education, like any other form of learning and development, calls for active participation on the part of the learner.

If you just *read* this book, few benefits will accrue. Even if you read it over and over again, not much change may be evident. Would you read a book on muscle building and expect to develop a good physique without actually performing the exercises? Of course not. The "psychological exercises" outlined throughout the following pages call for specific activity. This will consist of a deliberate rethinking of fallacious ideas and the subsequent systematic cultivation of different behaviors. Remember: well-meaning people have duped us into believing a mass of fallacies about how to lead satisfying and worthwhile lives. The time has come for change! And this takes work. *You can if you want to.*

We cannot overemphasize the importance of keeping careful records of the actual behaviors under scrutiny. You may consider it too mechanical and simplistic to jot down specific responses and to keep track of various thoughts and reactions. Don't! Those who make the most impressive psychological gains usually turn out to be the ones who take the trouble to chart their responses and to compute their daily or weekly averages. *So before you read any further, we suggest—in fact we really would like to insist—you purchase a pocket-size notebook in which you can record and tally the various reactions and interactions to which your attention will be drawn.* We would almost go so far as to say NO NOTEBOOK—NO CHANGE.

# Common Mistakes That Can Ruin Your Life—And How to Correct Them

What are the causes of emotional disturbance? Many diverse theories have been put forward. These range from "possession by evil spirits" to "repressed complexes and unconscious conflicts." In our view, the majority of "disturbed" people are not sick—just *mistaken.*

Emotional disturbance is essentially a result of *mistaken beliefs.* We are not helpless victims! There are no demons! What we need to do is identify and correct these mistaken beliefs—the common mistakes that can ruin our lives.

We have compiled a catalogue of 20 common mistakes, each of which is presented in the following format:

1. The mistake is identified.
2. A brief illustrative example is given.
3. Basic misconceptions which underlie the mistake are listed.

4. A program for change is outlined.

Make no mistake. These common errors in one way or another apply to virtually everyone—including you. Study them carefully and give them lots of thought. So, on to the specifics.

## MISTAKE #1: DON'T MAKE MISTAKES

**A junior business executive had many creative ideas that he repeatedly failed to mention at staff meetings because he was afraid he might be wrong and thus not be promoted. When the time came for evaluations, his employers regarded him as unimaginative and therefore did not promote him.**

***He believed (because he had been led to believe this all his life):***

1. People will think less of you if you make mistakes.
2. Making mistakes is a sign of weakness.
3. You appear stupid or foolish if you make mistakes.
4. If you make a mistake, try to cover it up.

DO *YOU* BELIEVE ANY OF THIS?

### HOW TO CHANGE

#### *A. Rethinking*

**1.** Consider the idea that to make mistakes can be beautiful, not simply tolerable, not merely acceptable, not only necessary, but actually desirable.

**2.** One of the major ways of learning is through mistakes. They provide clues for further growth.
**3.** Being right all the time is strongly anti-growth and in fact leads to the constant need to be on guard and to cover up. It leaves one tense and defensive.
**4.** Most people who observe mistakes will in fact be relieved to see that you are human, and a closer relationship will thus be possible. If someone puts you down, you won't be thrown by it when you realize that such criticism probably arises from the other person's insecurity.

### *B. Corrective Behavior*

**1.** Draw attention to some of the mistakes you make instead of covering them up. (We recognize that there are no absolute rules and that in certain situations it is necessary to cover up mistakes, but such situations are few and far between.)
**2.** Tell your friends about some of your major mistakes (it gets easier and even enjoyable as you practice it).
**3.** You might even deliberately go out of your way to make some minor mistakes.
**4.** In your pocket notebook, make a check mark every time you catch yourself covering up a mistake, or when you fail to take action for fear of making a mistake. Record each incident in a few words. Tally the total at the end of each week. (We ask you to keep a quantitative record of events because by becoming aware of your actions you automatically gain greater control over them.)
A page in your notebook might read like this:

| | *Covering up mistakes* | *Failing to take action* |
|---|---|---|
| Mon. | Forgot to call Jane—told her I tried many times but couldn't get through. | Didn't ask teacher to explain point. |
| Tues. | | |
| Wed. | Blamed the sun when I missed the tennis shot with Jim. | |
| Thurs. | Denied that I overslept, blamed traffic. | |
| Fri. | Argued with bank manager when I forgot to make deposit and was overdrawn. | Refused to play bridge because I wasn't as good as the others. |
| Sat. | | |
| Sun. | | Didn't challenge Gary's incorrect remark about what was wrong with the car. |
| Total: | *4* | 3 |

## MISTAKE #2: TRY TO BE GOOD AT EVERYTHING, OR PRETEND THAT YOU KNOW EVERYTHING

A gifted writer had won prizes for his short stories and for two plays. He had also invented several industrial appliances for which the patent rights earned him a large annual income. Yet he was extremely frustrated over the fact that poor coordination prevented him from excelling in sports and related physical skills.

***He believed:***

*1.* A worthwhile person is a good all-rounder. (S)he has a broad general knowledge coupled with a wide range of specific skills and talents.
*2.* Being beaten by others, and being no good at certain things or in certain situations, is a sign of stupidity and incompetence.
*3.* If you try hard enough you can excel at anything and everything.
*4.* To admit you don't know something, or to show that you cannot do something, is to display your basic inferiority.

DO *YOU* BELIEVE ANY OF THIS?

### HOW TO CHANGE

### *A. Rethinking*

**1.** Consider the reality that everyone has major limitations. If you are a good musician, a good carpenter, or a skillful mechanic, why get upset if you have no talent for painting, playing bridge, or if you cannot get the hang of doing crossword puzzles, solving math problems, playing golf, or whatever!

**2.** Most people aren't exceptionally good at anything. At best they do certain things well. A few people are fortunate (not better!) because they can do some things extremely well. In a complex and highly specialized society such as ours, it is impossible to have more than a vague working knowledge in most areas.

**3.** The idea that you can master anything if you really put your mind to it is absurd. It is also damaging, because many people waste their time and energy trying to prove the impossible to themselves and to others. The truth is that limitations imposed by genetic, temperamental, and constitutional factors, plus formative environmental events, preclude the acquisition of expertise in a wide array of human enterprises. Can everyone learn to write great literature? Can anyone become an outstanding athlete? Are attributes like perfect pitch, fine manual dexterity, special visual acuity, and so forth within everyone's grasp? Note: *I Can If I Want To* does not refer to growing wings, reaching seven feet in height, or being in New York and Los Angeles at the same time. It does refer to changing attitudes and behaviors that make us miserable.

**4.** Saying "I don't know" is more likely to earn respect for your integrity than disdain for your ignorance.

### *B. Corrective Behavior*

**1.** Observe the settings and situations in which you hesitate to say "I don't know," and where you actually pretend to be well-informed on a subject about which you know precious little. A common example is when someone mentions a book that you have not read, and you nod your head knowingly as if you've read it.

**2.** If there are times or places where you act like a know-it-all, try admitting your shortcomings or failings and see whether the results are generally in your favor. (We predict that other people will tend to like and trust you a good deal more.)

**3.** If you engage in social pastimes such as tennis or golf, do you behave as though a million dollars were at stake on every stroke? If so, deliberately tell yourself "it's only a game" and enjoy the mastery of trying to do *your* best (instead of *the* best) so that you genuinely enjoy yourself—win or lose.

**4.** In the notebook mark down the number of times you get upset when losing a game, as well as those times you feign competence and knowledge.

Initially, a typical week may look like this:

| | *Got upset* | *Pretended to know something* |
|---|---|---|
| Mon. | X X X | |
| Tues. | X X X X | X X |
| Wed. | X X | |
| Thurs. | X | |
| Fri. | X X X | X |
| Sat. | X | X X |
| Sun. | X X X | |

## *Illustrative Case*

A college student suffered from tension and anxiety. He attended group therapy to gain help with his problems. A pool table stood at one side of the large therapy room, and some members would play pool before and after the group sessions. The student was acutely upset whenever he missed a shot, especially an easy one. Another group member, by contrast, laughed good-naturedly at himself whenever he muffed a shot. In keeping with their different outlooks, whenever anyone in the group mentioned having played tennis, golf, or any other game, the student would ask, "Who won?" whereas the other group member always inquired, "Did you have fun?"

These different outlooks were discussed in the group and the young man was asked to practice Behavior Items # 3 and 4 of Mistake # 2.

A few months later, he was playing pool with the therapist. There was much fun and laughter, so much so that they forgot to keep score. At the end of the game, someone asked, "Who won?" The student replied, "We haven't the faintest idea, but we had a really great time!" This significant shift in outlook became evident in many areas of his life and the tension and anxiety soon disappeared.

## MISTAKE #3: THE LESS YOU DISCLOSE ABOUT YOURSELF THE BETTER OFF YOU WILL BE

**A young woman sought therapy because she felt depressed, lonely, and also suffered from feelings of "unreality." Her family had taught her to keep all her opinions to herself and to reveal as little as possible to other people.**

***She believed:***

1. If other people know what you are really like, they will automatically think less of you, if not actively dislike you.
2. Familiarity breeds contempt, so try to remain enigmatic and mysterious.
3. If people know intimate and personal facts about you, they will use this information against you.
4. The strong, silent type of person is a good model of mental health.

DO *YOU* BELIEVE ANY OF THIS?

### HOW TO CHANGE

### *A. Rethinking*

**1.** Consider very carefully the fact that close and meaningful friendships are impossible without mutual trust, mutual confidences, and personal revelations.

2. While it can be wise to keep your opinions to yourself in certain *work-related* situations (for example, it may not be prudent to tell your employer what you really think about him, or to discuss your innermost fears with fellow employees), it is most damaging to carry this guarded attitude into your marriage, your friendships, and other personal encounters.
3. Familiarity breeds contempt only among the contemptible! To avoid shared feelings and intimacies with significant others is to guarantee a lonely and detached existence.
4. The few people (and they are always very few) who may try to use personal information against you could never be "friends" (in the true sense) and are best dropped from your social circle. But try not to allow these few exploiters to deter you from being yourself and revealing yourself. Remember that one of the best ways of acquiring self-knowledge is by revealing yourself to others.
5. If you hide behind a facade and pretend to be what you think others want you to be, you will never know what it is like to be loved for what you really are.

### B. Corrective Behavior

1. Make a list of anything you have ever done, felt, or thought about, which you have never disclosed to *anyone*. Then try to decrease the items on this list—to zero if possible—by confiding selectively in trusted others. (This could be a large project, but you will find it to be extremely worthwhile.)

**2.** Take the risk of being a more open and self-disclosing person. Then see whether you find (as many of our colleagues, our patients, and we ourselves have found) that your dealings with other people become closer, more comfortable, and much deeper.
**3.** Put a mark in your notebook when you deliberately keep things to yourself. See how often you bury your true feelings, hide your honest opinions, and suppress your basic emotions. In most instances, the less you conceal, the better off you will be.

We are not asking you to give up being tactful or discreet when a situation demands it. *Don't make the mistake of overcompensation!* While correcting these common mistakes, it is easy for some people to think in terms of opposites and thus commit what might be termed the "converse error." Thus, "Don't make mistakes," becomes "Go out of your way to commit the most grievous errors in life." Mistake #2, "Try to be good at everything," is distorted into "Try to be good at nothing," and Mistake #3 (self-disclosure) becomes misconstrued as earnest advice to "spill one's guts" to all and sundry. Hopefully you will extract and apply the balanced perspectives that we intend to convey.

## Reminder

If you have been reading the foregoing pages without carrying out the prescribed behaviors, without actively changing your self-talk, and without deliberately disputing each of the false assumptions that may apply to you, this book will soon go the way of most self-help volumes. It will remain buried on a bedside table, or collect dust on a forgotten bookshelf.

## MISTAKE #4: YOU ARE A VICTIM OF CIRCUMSTANCES. YOUR LIFE IS BASICALLY CONTROLLED BY OUTSIDE FORCES

**A thirty-year-old man had tried several different jobs before giving up in disgust and becoming totally dependent for support on others. He came to therapy blaming bad luck and malicious employers and was envious of everyone who succeeded where he had failed.**

***He believed:***

1. What happens to you in life is largely under the control of others.
2. There is very little that you can do to change your destiny.
3. You are the way you are and you might as well accept it.
4. Your heredity and upbringing have made you what you are and you can do nothing to alter it.
5. Terrible things happen to you for which you are in no way responsible.

DO *YOU* BELIEVE ANY OF THIS?

### HOW TO CHANGE

#### *A. Rethinking*

**1.** Our lives unfold basically according to our own plans instead of just happening to us.

**2.** People have the capacity to change in the direction they wish.
**3.** In most areas of human interaction there are very few things you cannot do. There is almost no such thing as "can't," such as, "I can't stand up to my father." "I can't go in an elevator." "I can't lose weight." "I can't stop smoking." If you doubt it ask yourself the following questions:

*a.* If you were offered $10,000 in cash to do the thing you say you can't do, would you do it?
*b.* If someone pointed a gun at your head and threatened to kill you if you didn't do what you say you can't do, would you do it?
*c.* If a child of yours or the closest person to you in this world were kidnapped and you knew that you would never see this person alive again if you didn't do the thing you say you can't do, would you do it?

If the answer to any of these questions is "yes," then ask yourself "How is it that I won't do this for my own happiness?"
**4.** There are also very few things you "have to" do. People often say "I must or have to do something" when they actually mean "I choose to do it."

### *B. Corrective Behavior*

**1.** Write on a piece of paper one thing that you want to do, or something you want to change in yourself.
**2.** Make a plan to do it or change it. Examine step-by-step exactly what you can do to bring about the required change.

3. Every time you say "I can't," make a mark in your notebook.
4. Make a mark in the notebook every time you blame fate or someone else for your failures.

## A Case in Point

A middle-aged, obese man (5′8″ tall, 235 lb.) came for therapy expressing a desire to lose weight.

Step 1: Motivation was determined. Millions of people say they want to do something, but their every action contradicts the assertion. The man who came to us for therapy was obese because, like most other obese people, he decided that (*a*) the short-range pleasure of eating is more important than the long-range pleasure of being slim, and (*b*) the effort involved in losing weight and learning new eating patterns is more than he had wanted to invest.

Even if one's metabolism differs from that of most others, one still *can* lose weight. It is just a lot more difficult for some people than for others. Note that the statements "I want to, I'll try to, I think I will, it would be nice to, I ought to" are expressions of ambivalence and are instruments of SELF-DECEPTION. The only kind of statement that means anything in this context is "*I am going to go on a diet* starting now (or tomorrow morning at 8:00 A.M., etc.) and I am going to put in the necessary effort to accomplish the goal."

Step 2: When it was reasonably established that

our patient had genuinely made the decision to lose weight and that he was not kidding himself, the following technique proved useful. If you are interested in losing weight (or for that matter being able to do what you have mistakenly believed you cannot do) you too will find this technique extremely useful.

*a.* Decide how much weight you want to lose per week. In general, it is better to set a reasonable and not drastic figure, about two pounds.

*b.* Choose a fixed time every day to weigh yourself (the best time is probably first thing in the morning) and record the weights in your notebook.

*c.* Leave a sum of money much larger than you can afford to lose in cash with a friend or therapist. The friend checks your weight weekly. If at the end of one week you have not lost the specified amount of weight, the money is contributed to an organization you thoroughly detest along with a prewritten letter of praise. (For example, an extremely conservative Republican might cringe at the thought of sending a contribution and a letter of praise to a radical student group. A person who has always taken a strong pro-civil rights stand would be horrified at the thought of sending such a letter with contribution to a violently racist organization.) If the sum is large enough and the organization detestable enough, the chances are very great that you will lose the weight (or achieve many other goals that you may set for yourself). Once the weight has been lost, a similar system can prevent gaining it back. In the case mentioned, our patient shed fifty pounds in four months.

Notice that specific diets, which of course can be

very helpful, are not mentioned. The reason is that many people who seek diets are side-tracked from the major issue of motivation. Most people know *how* to lose weight—they just don't do it.

## MISTAKE #5: OTHER PEOPLE ARE HAPPY

**A man of twenty-six who had very little social life was quite depressed. On a spring day while glancing out of the therapist's office he commented: "Look at all those happy couples walking arm in arm. What have I got? No love, no happiness, nothing. Why am I so lonely and miserable? Why me?"**

***He believed:***

1. You can tell people's inner feelings from their outward appearances.
2. People who say they are happy are indeed happy.
3. Most other people are normal. "They may have problems but not like mine."
4. People who have extrinsic marks of success (wealth, fame, good looks) are happy, or happier than people who don't.
5. "I wish I were somebody else."

DO *YOU* BELIEVE ANY OF THIS?

### HOW TO CHANGE

#### *A. Rethinking*

**1.** In most instances it is not true that other people are happy. *You simply assume that they are.*
**2.** Everyone has problems, hangups, limitations, inse-

curities (a majority serious enough to interfere with their functioning in a significant way), and virtually everyone in this world has at some time been depressed and even had suicidal thoughts.

**3.** Almost everyone goes through a private hell but because of barriers to self-disclosure and the shame of admitting limitations, you rarely hear about it.

**4.** Tens of millions of people live under conditions of incredible hardship—poverty, starvation, illness, and deformities of all kinds.

**5.** Where are all the happy people? Many come to therapists saying "I am envied, I have everything that anyone would want, but I am miserable." The following famous American poem illustrates the point:

Whenever Richard Cory went down town,
  We people on the pavement looked at him:
He was a gentleman from sole to crown,
  Clean favored, and imperially slim.

And he was always quietly arrayed,
  And he was always human when he talked;
But still he fluttered pulses when he said,
  "Good-morning," and he glittered when he walked.

And he was rich—yes, richer than a king,
  And admirably schooled in every grace:
In fine, we thought that he was everything
  To make us wish that we were in his place.

So on we worked, and waited for the light,
  And went without the meat, and cursed the bread;
And Richard Cory, one calm summer night,
  Went home and put a bullet through his head.

Edwin Arlington Robinson

***B. Corrective Behavior***

**1.** When walking in the street, using public transportation, or while at work or at school, look at other people's expressions. Have your observations been correct about how happy other people *look*?
**2.** Ask people you know very well (friends, relatives) if they are happy. If they say yes, ask what makes it that way for them. If not, ask what is missing. How would you rate them now on a minus five to plus five scale? (−5 would signify extreme unhappiness, 0 would be neutral, and +5 would denote great joy.)
**3.** Look for faults, problems, limitations, hangups, and suffering in those you think are happy in order to get a balanced perspective. *Write your findings in the notebook.*

## Read This Now

When you read the various points we have outlined under RETHINKING, we assume that you will not browse through them, but that you will study them and reread some of them several times. Remember: no browsing! The process of RETHINKING calls for active thought and contemplation. We suggest that you go back right now and reread all the points in the preceding mistakes and ponder each one. Change involves *active* reading of the material, not a passive process of silent or cursory contact.

*I CAN IF I WANT TO*

The sections on CORRECTIVE BEHAVIOR clearly call for specific actions, things to *do* in order to change. Again, if all you do is read about the new behaviors and if you do not practice them, significant gains are not likely to follow.

Once more this is a reminder that it is your life and your happiness that are at stake. You can change —even in a short time. Skimpy reading is a self-deception. This is a *work book.* Study it. We are supplying the tools. The rest is up to you.

*Arnold Lazarus/Allen Fay*

# MISTAKE #6: LET YOUR ANGER OUT

**A twenty-eight-year-old divorced woman had attended encounter groups for many months in the hope of becoming less inhibited and having a more fulfilled social life. In the groups she had learned that it was unhealthy to keep anger in and was trained to express it. However, she was no happier and, in fact, the few people with whom she had previously been fairly close were beginning to find her offensive.**

***She believed:***

1. It is perfectly normal and healthy to get angry.
2. When you feel angry, it is good for you to express it freely.
3. When you are frustrated or displeased by someone, it is advisable to vent your anger and tell him or her off.
4. Yelling and screaming at other people gives you the upper hand.

DO *YOU* BELIEVE ANY OF THIS?

## HOW TO CHANGE

### *A. Rethinking*

**1.** There is a difference between experiencing feelings of anger and the outward expression of rage toward another person.
**2.** One can express displeasure more constructively by a direct statement rather than by an emotional out-

burst. Direct statement: "I would really appreciate it if you would put your underwear in the hamper instead of on the bedroom floor." Angry statement: "Why the hell do you leave your goddam underwear strewn all over the bedroom? You're a disgusting slob!"

**3.** There is a difference between getting angry and being assertive.

**4.** *Getting* angry usually involves a loss of control. (This is different from voluntarily giving up control.)

**5.** Getting angry is simply a discharge of emotions and does not lead to growth. You might sometimes feel better for the moment, though you are just as likely to remain upset. Many people, in fact, feel frightened that they have lost control.

**6.** People who often get angry are usually unassertive. Getting angry is generally an acknowledgment of failure to cope with or solve a problem. Note the difference between *assertion* and *aggression*. Assertion involves taking a stand, resisting unreasonable demands, or asking for what you want. Aggression involves putting another person down. Assertion is positive, aggression negative.

### *B. Corrective Behavior*

**1.** Practice behaving more assertively. Again, assertive behaviors would include asking for something you want (for example, a salary raise or a date with someone you find appealing), initiating conversations, saying "no" to unreasonable or unwanted requests, telling others honestly what you think of their opinions, appearance or actions (positive and negative).

**2.** Monitor your unassertive behavior. Each time you

are less assertive than you might have been, jot down the incident in your notebook.

**3.** If you are fighting a lot with family, close friends, a lover, etc., make a notation in your book each time a fight occurs. If arguments occur at home, post a chart on the inside of a closet door and record the date, time, and duration of each fight.

**4.** If the fighting persists, set aside a period of two minutes for a contrived fight at a fixed time each day. Use a timer (if you don't have one, it's a worthwhile investment), and set it for two minutes. During that period of time, yell at each other, curse each other, and go beyond anything you might say in a spontaneous fight. At the end of the two minutes—that is, when the timer goes off, STOP IMMEDIATELY and hug one another. If you want to continue fighting after that, it's up to you but it is essential to have at least a five-minute break between the exercise and any other fighting. (Note that this fighting is controlled; it is a deliberately planned exercise and very different from spontaneous aggressiveness.)

**5.** For those with more energy, a two-minute pillow fight is recommended.

**6.** Each time you feel intimidated by someone else's anger, say to yourself: "This person is probably feeling very threatened and insecure." Practice responding in one of the following ways:

*a. Supportively* ("I am sorry you are upset. Can I do anything to make you feel better?")

*b. Assertively* ("Please talk to me nicely.")

*c. Non-reinforcingly* (By ignoring the person when he yells and being very attentive when he talks reasonably.)

*d. Paradoxically* (By absurdly agreeing with his irrationality, for example, "You are absolutely right. I never realized how colossally stupid I am. If there were more people like me, the human species wouldn't survive.")

**7.** If you do actually find yourself in a battle, say to yourself or to the other person, "Stop! This is crazy!"

**8.** After every angry outburst or feeling, say to yourself, "What result did I want and how could I have better achieved it?"

**9.** During a fight say to yourself, "What would I feel like if I were the other person?" When you get a chance, write out the answer to the question.

**10.** Look at other people who are angry. Do you want to be that way?

# MISTAKE #7: YOU SHOULD FEEL GUILTY IF YOU DO YOUR OWN THING AND OTHERS ARE UPSET BY IT

**A young married couple visited the husband's parents every Sunday. The visits usually were unpleasant. Each Sunday morning, in anticipation of a miserable day, the couple would be at each other's throats. They wished to visit less frequently but felt guilty about hurting the parents' feelings.**

***They believed:***

1. It is bad to act in your own interest when people might be offended or their feelings hurt.
2. If others didn't like a particular action or statement of yours, they might dislike you, and that would be terrible.
3. If you don't do what the other person wants, you will lose his/her love, and that would also be terrible.
4. It is better to give than to receive.

DO *YOU* BELIEVE ANY OF THIS?

## HOW TO CHANGE

### *A. Rethinking*

**1.** In the vast majority of instances you don't hurt others' feelings. They upset themselves through their own interpretation of the event. There are many possible ways of reacting to the same situation.

**2.** When other people are truly interested in your growth and happiness as well as their own, you and they will be better off if they don't pressure you or coerce you.

**3.** If you act in your own interest, others will respect you more and your own self-esteem will be higher than if you do other people's bidding and see yourself as trapped or coerced.

**4.** If assertiveness and honesty result in the loss of the other person's love, it wasn't love.

**5.** When you think of what is good for you, try to consider long-term advantages as well as short-term benefits. In other words, apart from immediate satisfactions, take into account how your actions will affect you a month from now or a year from now.

**6.** Neither giving nor receiving is better. It is best to give and to receive.

### *B. Corrective Behavior*

**1.** If you are the kind of person who says "yes" routinely no matter how you feel, practice saying, "Let me think about it." "I'll let you know." "I'll call you back."

**2.** Record in your notebook each instance when you are less assertive than you might have been. One day's record might look like this:

*November 17*

1. Allowed Janet to talk me into going to the party, wanted early night—knew would be bored.

2. Tried to return scratched record. Backed down when salesperson said I must have damaged it.
3. Told Marge I thought her new dress was beautiful—really I thought it was hideous.

**3.** Rehearse a more assertive response when you are alone, either aloud or silently. Then write out a brief script of what actually occurred, followed by a more assertive version. For example, sample scripts of the preceding incidents might read as follows:

*a. Actual Incident*

Janet: I really wish you would come with me to the party.

Me: Well, I'm kind of tired and would rather not.

Janet: I know you'll have a good time. And anyhow, the Johnsons will be very hurt if you don't go.

Me: Oh, well, okay.

*Corrected Script*

Janet: I really wish you would come with me to the party.

Me: Well, I'm kind of tired and have decided not to go.

Janet: I know you'll have a good time. And anyhow, the Johnsons will be very hurt if you don't go.

Me: I hope that the Johnsons will not be offended, but I am very tired and am going to have an early night. You go and have a good time.

*b. Actual Incident*

Me: I bought this record here two days ago

| | |
|---|---|
| | and noticed that it was scratched when I played it on my phonograph. |
| Salesperson: | Our records are sealed at the factory and there's no way that they can get scratched. It must have happened when you played it. |
| Me: | Well, I noticed it as soon as I put on the phonograph. |
| Salesperson: | There must be something wrong with your needle. I'm sorry, we can't take it back. |
| Me: | That's the last time you'll see me here! (Walked out feeling upset.) |

*Corrected Script*

| | |
|---|---|
| Salesperson: | . . . It must have happened when you played it. |
| Me: | No way! I know how to handle records. This record was defective, and I either want to exchange it for another one or get a cash refund. |

c. *Actual Incident*

Marge: How do you like my new dress?
Me: It's gorgeous, really terrific.

*Corrected Script*

Marge: How do you like my new dress?
Me: I don't like this particular dress.

or

We sure differ on this one. I don't like it at all.

or

This one doesn't do justice to your figure or bring out your coloring.

*Arnold Lazarus/Allen Fay*

## A Note About Assertive Behavior

The importance of making direct and honest statements and the value of standing up for your rights can hardly be overemphasized. Please note that the assertive person does not always get what he/she wants, but at least she/he has the satisfaction of having taken affirmative action. The cultivation of a direct, open, honest, and forthright expression of what you feel and think will spare you untold anguish, and a variety of problems or symptoms.

## MISTAKE #8: MAKE SURE THAT YOU PLEASE OTHER PEOPLE AND THAT THEY LIKE AND APPROVE OF YOU

A young woman who went out of her way to please everybody and to win affection found herself in a difficult position when several intimate friends would make conflicting demands. Of course, her own needs were never expressed, and she began to experience anxiety and panic attacks.

*She believed:*

1. It is better to please other people than to please yourself.
2. If you constantly go out of your way to please other people, they will like and respect you.
3. Putting other people's needs before your own will permit you to count on them when you need them.
4. If you do not please other people you are hurting your chances for happiness and fulfillment.

DO *YOU* BELIEVE ANY OF THIS?

### HOW TO CHANGE

### *A. Rethinking*

**1.** People who try to please everybody tend to end up being nothing to themselves. When you are nothing to yourself, how can you be something to anyone else?
**2.** People who do not act in their own interest do not

seem "real," and others tend to be very uncomfortable around them.

**3.** People tend to respect enlightened self-interest and disrespect self-downing behavior. (There is a difference between self-interest and selfishness. Enlightened self-interest implies that one considers his/her impact upon others. Selfishness involves disregarding the effects of one's actions on others.)

**4.** Even if you could please everyone, you would be in a vulnerable position. As soon as someone showed displeasure you would be completely thrown because you would not have acquired appropriate ways of responding to even the mildest criticism. Learning how to risk others' displeasure and how to deal with it when it does occur is a necessary part of growth. Secondly, when you fail to express an opinion for fear of displeasing others, you are bound to remain alienated from yourself.

(This mistake reminds us of the story about two friends who were regular churchgoers. Whereas one was rather casual about his prayers, the other was intent upon pleasing God, praising Him, and generally going out of his way to be "religious." Yet the casual man fared well and became prosperous and happy while his serious-minded friend kept struggling along despite even greater attempts to please the Lord. Finally, when the latter turned to God and asked why all his sacrifices and prayers had gone unheeded, God answered: "Because you bug me!")

### *B. Corrective Behavior*

**1.** Practice doing more things to please yourself, even when this sometimes runs counter to the needs of others.

2. In each and every situation where decisions are made, try to think "What would be best for me?" and write this choice in a notebook. If you are not sure what is best for you, make a list of pros and cons.
3. If you have already made a hasty decision, go back over it and see how you might have done it differently. Rehearse in your mind, or with another person, the more positive behavior.
4. Put a mark in the notebook each time you please someone else at your own expense. At the end of the day get the total and try to come up with various ways of lowering your score.

Note: This discussion should not be misconstrued as implying that pleasing others per se is a mistake. Many of us derive genuine pleasure from pleasing others. We are referring to "people pleasers" who inappropriately put others' needs before their own.

## MISTAKE #9: BE RIGHT. SHOW OTHERS THAT YOUR OPINIONS ARE BETTER THAN THEIRS

**A thirty-five-year-old woman was troubled by unsatisfactory relationships, socially and at work. In fact, she had no real friends. It was noted that she spoke with great certainty about everything and often when someone disagreed with her, she would say things like, "Utter nonsense" or "That's ridiculous."**

***She believed:***

1. I *think* I know, therefore I do know.
2. My opinion is not just my opinion but a fact.
3. It is important that my opinion be right. Otherwise I look like a fool.
4. When I present my views, if I don't act as if I'm right, people won't respect me.

DO *YOU* BELIEVE ANY OF THIS?

### HOW TO CHANGE

### *A. Rethinking*

**1.** There is a big difference between fact and truth on the one hand, and belief, opinion, taste, and preference on the other.

**2.** A fact can be tested or checked: Lincoln was born in 1809. A belief, opinion, taste, or preference cannot: corn tastes better than peas, long hair is more attractive than short hair.

3. Every person has the right to express his opinion without being ridiculed or shouted down.
4. Differences of opinion and one's tolerance of these differences lead to growth.
5. It is important to avoid attacking or labeling those who disagree with us. There is a significant difference between what is wrong and what we dislike or disapprove of. There is no such thing as wrong or immoral thinking or behavior unless it can be shown that it results in harm to other people.

### *B. Corrective Behavior*

1. When not dealing with clear-cut facts, practice saying "It seems to me, it is my impression, I think, I believe, it is my opinion . . ." rather than "I know, it is a fact, it is certain," etc.
2. Monitor this trait in others as well as in yourself. Record with a check mark in the notebook every dogmatic statement you make: "You are wrong, I am right, you have no taste, you don't know what's good, you have no brains."
3. Politely correct this type of communication in others. For example, if someone says "You have no taste," you respond nicely with "You mean you disagree with what I said."
4. Practice disagreeing constructively with others: "This may be a great painting but I don't particularly like it."
5. If you are not accustomed to thinking about the difference between fact and belief, make a mental note each time you have a discussion or dispute as to whether the issue is an "f" issue (fact) or a "b" issue (belief).

*Arnold Lazarus/Allen Fay*

## MISTAKE #10: YOU MUST EARN HAPPINESS

**A middle-aged man's puritanical background led him to believe that he was not entitled to happiness or feelings of joy unless he first did something productive, creative, or worthwhile. Whenever he felt spontaneous feelings of pleasure or contentment (which was not too often!) he immediately beçame guilty and anxious, unless he was able to justify his good feelings.**

***He believed:***

*1.* The purpose of life is to work hard and to be productive—not happy.
*2.* Those who value happiness are self-indulgent pleasure-seekers who will never get ahead.
*3.* Beware of pleasure and happiness, for it is always followed by pain and misery.
*4.* If you are unhappy in this life you have a better chance of true happiness in the hereafter.
DO *YOU* BELIEVE ANY OF THIS?

### HOW TO CHANGE

#### *A. Rethinking*

**1.** Consider the proposition that happiness is a birthright. You are alive, therefore you are entitled to happiness.
**2.** Remember that too many people who faithfully follow the prescription to work hard, sacrifice, achieve,

accomplish, create, and get ahead either "crack up" in the process or find an emotional vacuum at the end of it all. They also attempt to induce guilt in others. YOU ARE ENTITLED TO DO WHATSOEVER PLEASES YOU, PROVIDED YOU DO NOT HARM ANYONE ELSE IN THE PROCESS. (We see morality in the context of relationships and thus feel that if you harm only yourself, it may be unfortunate but not immoral.)

### *B. Corrective Behavior*

**1.** Record in the notebook how much of your time is spent doing what you think you "should" be doing as opposed to what you would really enjoy doing. (At the end of each day make an estimate of "enjoyment" hours and "duty" hours.)
**2.** Spend at least one hour per day doing something for "pure pleasure." (Take care here that your pleasure-activities do not conflict with another goal. For example, if you wish to lose weight, do not choose an hour's worth of eating for your "pure pleasure.")
**3.** Make a list of those things that have been fun for you, or could be fun. Systematically try to inject more and more of these "fun things" into your daily activities. For example, if you enjoy concerts, plays, dances, swimming, painting, bowling, reading, warm showers, playing cards, taking hikes, having intercourse, masturbating, visiting friends, taking photographs, etc., increase doing whatever turns you on.
**4.** For one week, at the end of each day, rate individual activities on a scale of −5 to +5 (where −5 would be extreme displeasure, 0 would be neutral and +5 would signify extreme joy). Total your score and see if you

are comfortably in the + column. For example one of our patients gave the following rating: Waking up (−1), Shaving (0), Showering (+1), Driving to work (−1), Attending to customers (−2), Meeting with friends for lunch (+3), Dictating letters (0), Checking invoices (−1), Meeting with buyers (+2), Driving home (+2), Having dinner (+2), Visiting in-laws (0). Thus, his score for that day was +5. How could he have scored at least +10?

## MISTAKE #11: PLAY IT SAFE. DON'T TAKE RISKS

**A forty-eight-year-old druggist who worked in a hospital dispensary was distressed over the fact that he had missed the opportunity to open a drugstore with one of his friends. "I felt secure working in the hospital and didn't want to take any chances. My friend then asked someone else to join him in the venture, and one year later they opened up two new branches."**

***He believed:***

1. It is vital to check and recheck everything and to look very carefully before you leap.
2. Play it close to home and you won't get hurt.
3. Whenever you take any chances or risks you are only looking for trouble.
4. Security is more important than happiness.

DO *YOU* BELIEVE ANY OF THIS?

### HOW TO CHANGE

***A. Rethinking***

**1.** Very often, when you keep "looking before you leap" you end up "missing the boat." It is wise to give careful consideration to certain matters, but sometimes, when you "leap before you look," you may "hit the jackpot."

**2.** Life itself entails a series of risks each and every

moment. The wise individual will obviously avoid dangerous or harmful situations, but the risks to which we are referring do not fall into this category. Taking calculated *psychological* risks (such as accepting a new job, telling someone off, going out on a blind date, asking a favor, expressing an opinion, or offering advice) tends to change an everyday existence into an exciting life.

**3.** The old philosophy—nothing ventured, nothing gained—underscores the fact that those people who avoid psychological risk-taking gain nothing but loneliness and frustration. Many people who feel alone in this world do not venture out of their ruts but keep hoping that by some stroke of fortune, good things will just happen to come their way.

**4.** Do you know *anyone* who leads a happy and fulfilling life who does not take risks?

### *B. Corrective Behavior*

**1.** Ask yourself: "What can I start doing that I have avoided doing?" Then take the risk of doing some of these specific things; for example, asking for a raise, asking for a date, inviting someone over, revealing an intimate feeling, or expressing a different point of view.

**2.** Take at least one psychological risk each day. Jot it down. (Example: "I spoke back to my uncle." "I refused to work overtime." "I asked a friend to pay back the money he owed me.") At the end of a week, if you have taken 7 or more risks, you will probably have more self-confidence and a feeling of being in greater control of your own destiny.

## An Illustrative Case History

This is a good point in time for you to study a case history that illustrates how you can change your behavior if you want to!

A young man was very timid about asking women out. He was terrified of being rejected and would not take the risk of initiating any contact. We suggested the following steps:

1. For one week he was to record every opportunity he had to talk to a woman to whom he felt at least slightly attracted (at work, in elevators, stores, restaurants, bars, museums, parks, the laundry room, etc.). This included situations where he was near a woman for at least a few seconds (more than passing very quickly in the street). The first week looked like this:

| Mon. | Tues. | Wed. | Thurs. | Fri. | Sat. | Sun. |
|---|---|---|---|---|---|---|
| 𝍷𝍷 | 𝍷 | 𝍸 | 𝍷 | 0 | 𝍸 𝍷𝍷 | 𝍷𝍷 |

2. Next, he was asked to assign points to these encounters, using the following scale: *0* if he said nothing; *1* if he smiled and made a casual remark, such as "Hi" or "Nice day" or "That's a nice sweater you are wearing"; *2* if he had at least a short conversation where the woman responded and he continued the discussion, even briefly; *3* if he asked to see her or for her phone number. (It made no difference if he was turned down. The only important issue was asking.)

For each possible encounter he could have received a maximum of three points. For example, in the record above he could have had 6 points on Monday, 3 on Tuesday, 15 on Wednesday, etc. The second week looked like this:

| | Mon. | Tues. | Wed. | Thurs. | Fri. | Sat. | Sun. |
|---|---|---|---|---|---|---|---|
| Maximum possible points | 6 | 9 | 6 | 15 | 6 | 6 | 3 |
| Actual points received | 0 | 2 | 2 | 4 | 2 | 3 | 1 |

You can see that this is not an all-or-none concept. It is valuable to get practice simply chatting for a while even without asking for a date. By monitoring this behavior over a period of time, the young man was greeting every woman he wanted to and his actual score began to approach the maximum. As he became more comfortable saying "Hi" (a 1-point rating), brief conversations (2 points) soon followed. The latter increased in frequency over the next couple of months, by which time he was having a fairly active social life.

## MISTAKE #12: TRY TO BECOME TOTALLY INDEPENDENT AND SELF-SUFFICIENT

**A young man who boasted that he "did not need anyone for anything" also stated that he could see no value, no purpose, and no meaning to life.**

***He believed:***

*1.* To need someone's help or assistance automatically places you in a vulnerable position.
2. It is always good to compete and win so that you are one-up.
*3.* You are either a self-reliant and independent person or you are a weak and immature underling.
*4.* Turning to someone else for advice or assistance is to admit your own ineptitude and to display your limitations.

DO *YOU* BELIEVE ANY OF THIS?

### HOW TO CHANGE

### *A. Rethinking*

**1.** There is a world of difference between "healthy" and "parasitic" dependency. In our complex society, we are all dependent on others to a greater or lesser extent. Most people do not build their own houses, grow their own food, or make their own clothes. Nor can they repair such things as their own TV sets and cars. Dentists don't usually try to fill their own cavities!

**2.** The Annie-get-your-gun philosophy ("I can do anything you can do better!") runs counter to basic psychology. Everyone, with the exception of identical twins, has different genes and chromosomes and we all have different social learning experiences. Thus, virtually every person must have some knowledge, skill, or talent that you do not possess (and vice versa). To pretend otherwise is to rob yourself of the opportunity to benefit from the other person's unique capacities.

**3.** By adopting a competitive attitude ("I can do anything as well as, or better than you!") as opposed to a cooperative attitude ("There must be certain things you know and can do that I don't know and can't do!") you create distance, antagonism, suspicion, defensiveness, and ill-will.

**4.** When people pool their resources they are mutually strengthened ("I'll help you out in those areas where I know more than you and would appreciate assistance from you in those situations where you know more than I.") Successful marriages, for instance, are predicated upon mutual sharing, whereas competition between spouses is generally corrosive.

### *B. Corrective Behavior*

**1.** Make a notation in your book each time you need assistance but are too proud or too inhibited to ask for it.

**2.** Practice asking small favors of others. As with most things, it is difficult at first but soon becomes much easier.

**3.** Practice accepting compliments and saying "thank you" instead of dismissing them or putting yourself down.

**4.** Remember that it pays to achieve a balance between dependent and independent behaviors. The hermit who is supposedly completely independent is hardly a model of human adjustment. Review the things you do for yourself and the things you ask others to do for you *each day.*

## MISTAKE #13: IF YOU AVOID PROBLEMS AND UNPLEASANT SITUATIONS THEY WILL DISAPPEAR IN TIME

**A woman complained of chronic unhappiness. Throughout her childhood and adolescence, whenever she experienced problems or expressed anger, her mother would say "Go and lie down, dear, and you will feel better." She learned to "sweep things under the rug" and to avoid any direct confrontations with others.**

***She believed:***

*1.* Many unpleasant situations only get worse when you face up to them.
*2.* If you leave distressing things alone and turn a deaf ear, they tend to go away.
*3.* If you keep saying "Everything will be all right," this positive thinking will be most helpful.
*4.* It is a sign of good breeding and civilized living to ignore disagreeable issues.

DO *YOU* BELIEVE ANY OF THIS?

### HOW TO CHANGE

### *A. Rethinking*

**1.** The tendency to engage in excessive avoidance is probably the most obvious sign of "neurotic" behavior. **2.** Taking the "easy" way out often proves to be more taxing in the long run. When you avoid most problems, they do not disappear but often loom larger.

**3.** Being inhibited and indirect in the name of tact and diplomacy results in hypocritical and phony life-styles.

### *B. Corrective Behavior*

**1.** Make a list of any problem areas or unpleasant situations that you have been avoiding, for example, telling your spouse to stop smothering you; asking your in-laws to offer less gratuitous advice, requesting a friend to pay back money, asking someone to go out with you, writing a letter of complaint, visiting a friend in the hospital.

**2.** Picture yourself successfully carrying out these actions. Rehearse what you will say and how you will say it. If you have a tape recorder, record your imaginary dialogue and listen to playbacks. You'll find this very helpful.

**3.** Take small steps at a time. Begin by confronting those issues that are easiest for you, and then systematically increase the difficulty of the tasks you set for yourself. Keep notes of those situations and events you formerly avoided but which you are now progressively approaching.

# MISTAKE #14: STRIVE FOR PERFECTION

**A young actress set such high standards for herself that she constantly failed to live up to her own expectations. She often felt frustrated, anxious, depressed, and thoroughly inadequate.**

***She believed:***

*1.* If you can't do something perfectly, you might as well not do it at all.
*2.* To strive for anything less than perfection is to be a second-class human being.
*3.* Many people have perfect marriages, perfect children, perfect parents, perfect jobs, perfect friendships, etc.
*4.* It is indeed possible to be a perfect wife or husband, a perfect son or daughter, a perfect employer or employee, etc.

DO *YOU* BELIEVE ANY OF THIS?

## HOW TO CHANGE

### *A. Rethinking*

**1.** If your level of aspiration is too high, you will often defeat your own purposes. Strive for competence, but since perfection seldom exists, you will get a lot further by aiming to do things well instead of seeking perfection.

**2.** To insist upon perfection in yourself or in others is bound to cause unhappiness and disappointment because you and everyone else will constantly fall short of the mark.

**3.** If you accept the fact that all human beings, *by their very nature*, are imperfect and fallible, you will strive to be less imperfect and less fallible, but you will never try to be (or pretend to be) perfect or infallible.

**4.** The process of trying to do something well often proves enjoyable, but when reaching for perfection, each step along the way is fraught with tension and anxiety.

### *B. Corrective Behavior*

**1.** Make a list of the things you have quit because you didn't do them perfectly. Then resume some of these abandoned activities for sheer enjoyment. (Some people stop playing the piano, or avoid sex, or give up tennis, or sketching, or dancing, etc., because they cannot perform well enough, or achieve perfection.) This is very foolish behavior. IT PAYS TO GET PLEASURE FROM THE ACTIVITY REGARDLESS OF THE END RESULT.

**2.** Work at developing an anti-perfectionistic outlook. Explain to other people why perfectionism is self-defeating, and jot down all the drawbacks of perfectionism.

## MISTAKE #15: YOU CAN DRAW GENERAL CONCLUSIONS ABOUT PEOPLE FROM INDIVIDUAL STATEMENTS OR ACTIONS

**A mechanical engineer came for therapy because he was bored, lonely, and frustrated. He had no close friends and had been a loner most of his life. It soon became obvious that he was both self-critical and overcritical of others. He was quick to judge others and to find them wanting, and he was extremely hard on himself. When he learned to stop condemning *people* and to criticize only their specific *behaviors*—and when he learned to separate his own specific behaviors from his basic personality—many productive and profound changes soon became evident.**

***He believed:***

1. If someone performs a selfish, aggressive, or dishonest act, this makes him/her a selfish, aggressive, or dishonest person.
2. If someone has some hostile, nasty, or crazy thoughts, this automatically makes that individual a hostile and nasty human being.
3. If you put someone else down—for example, by picking out his shortcomings—this generally places you in a one-up position.
4. You can tell a lot about people from their occupations, the kinds of cars they drive, the types of clothes they wear, etc.

DO *YOU* BELIEVE ANY OF THIS?

## HOW TO CHANGE

### *A. Rethinking*

**1.** First and foremost, separate individual, specific actions from total *personality.* A person who displays a few selfish and aggressive behaviors may have many very desirable qualities.
**2.** To label others (or yourself) is inaccurate and potentially destructive. If you say "He is a thief," when you could have said "He stole a loaf of bread," you are labeling. If, on the other hand you say "He told a lie," rather than "He is a liar," you are simply making a statement.
**3.** If someone has a very desirable trait, that does not automatically make that individual a desirable person.
**4.** Think about some of your failures and some of the foolish things you have said and done, and try to realize that this does not make you "a failure" or "a fool."

### *B. Corrective Behavior*

**1.** Monitor the number of times you are aware of putting *yourself* down instead of criticizing a particular behavior ("I am stupid" instead of "I did a stupid thing.")
**2.** Try to catch yourself whenever you put someone else down as opposed to commenting on that person's behavior ("He is a bastard" instead of "He said some nasty things.")
**3.** Acquire the habit of refusing to pass judgment on others. If you conclude from first impressions that a

person is arrogant, snobbish, etc., make an effort to talk to that person and get to know her/him.

**4.** Whenever anyone makes a judgment about you—for example, "I think you are a hostile person"—be sure to explain that while you may appear hostile from time to time, you can also be very loving. Emphasize that to be a "hostile person" one would have to be hostile most of the time.

## MISTAKE #16: SOME PEOPLE ARE BETTER THAN OTHERS

**A young woman who worked for a New York advertising agency tended to feel utterly worthless and depressed when meeting the many attractive, bright, wealthy people with whom she came into daily contact. She disregarded the fact that she was warm, kind, and honest, but assumed that most people were that way and that these qualities were less important.**

***She believed:***

1. Individuals with high intelligence, good looks, money, athletic ability, creative talent, power, and prestige are better people than those without these attributes.
2. These attributes make one happy.
3. Without these qualities it is very difficult to be happy.
4. People really respect only those who possess these extrinsic qualities.

DO *YOU* BELIEVE ANY OF THIS?

### HOW TO CHANGE

### *A. Rethinking*

**1.** Although some people may possess superior skills in one or even in many areas, this does not make them superior human beings. Everyone has faults, limitations, and insecurities, as well as assets.

**2.** There are no superior human beings—not royalty, heads of state, religious leaders, heads of large corporations, famous actors, athletes, doctors, lawyers, or teachers.
**3.** Be aware that most people who feel like losers do not know the private agonies of the so-called "superior beings."
**4.** The superior/inferior idea is dangerous. People who are considered superior often become arrogant and seek and abuse power over others.
**5.** It is just as damaging to think you are superior as it is to think you are inferior. People who think they are superior often find it difficult, if not impossible, to learn from others, or to profit from their own mistakes.

### *B. Corrective Behavior*

**1.** When you are with someone to whom you feel inferior, actively say to yourself: "This person can do x, y, and z better than I can, but that does not make her or him a superior person."
**2.** Instead of getting into a competitive frame of mind, look for good intrinsic qualities in the other person (for example, kindness, compassion, warmth, or humor) that enable you to like that individual. After being with a "superior" person jot down in a notebook any intrinsic positive qualities they may possess.
**3.** Above all, do not shy away from "superiors" as if you were unworthy of their time. Whenever possible, seek out their company and take the risk of stating your own opinions and airing your views. Jot down the number of times per week that you make such contact.
**4.** Make a mark in your notebook each time you have

an "inferiority" thought. Add up the daily total and keep an ongoing record. (You will discover that keeping a record of negative events will help you to gain control over them.)

## MISTAKE #17: THE "EITHER/OR" MISTAKE

**A strongly partisan politician became progressively more mistrustful of others' motives and loyalties. His philosophy had always been "Either you're with me or agin me!" He began to perceive innocent questions as virulent attacks and became depressed when he realized that he had lost many would-be supporters.**

***He believed:***

1. Generally speaking, you can divide the world into friendly and unfriendly people, the honest and dishonest, the decent and indecent, etc.
2. Most things are either black or white, that is good-bad, right-wrong, worthwhile-worthless, and the like.
3. Concerning yourself, you are either a success or a failure, liked or disliked, clever or stupid, attractive or unattractive.

DO *YOU* BELIEVE ANY OF THIS?

### HOW TO CHANGE

#### *A. Rethinking*

**1.** In the domain of human relationships, virtually everything falls on a continuum.
**2.** Try to realize that almost any dichotomy—honest-dishonest, introverted-extroverted, normal-abnormal, sensitive-insensitive—is bound to be false because the

vast majority of people fall somewhere in the middle.
3. Since no trait exists in pure form, everyone is a mixture of many different attributes and many gradations within each area.

### *B. Corrective Behavior*

1. Acquire a keen awareness of your own dichotomous reasoning. Whenever you catch yourself arbitrarily making "good-bad," "right-wrong" statements, make a check mark in your notebook.
2. A useful assertive response is to make others aware of their own dichotomous reasoning.

# MISTAKE #18: PERFORMING WELL IS IMPORTANT FOR FULFILLMENT

**A young man came for help because he was very discouraged about his sex-life. After many repeated failures at achieving an erection he had withdrawn from sexual contact. In his dealings with people he was always eager to impress them.**

***He believed:***

1. The measure of your worth is reflected by the adequacy of your performance.
2. Poor performance will lead others to think little of you, and the opinion of other people is very important.
3. People will like you and respect you if you are a superstar.
4. The harder you strive to perform, the better you will do.

DO *YOU* BELIEVE ANY OF THIS?

## HOW TO CHANGE

### *A. Rethinking*

**1.** If you concentrate on having fun instead of worrying about your image, many things will work out better for you.
**2.** In many instances, by striving to perform well, you will only succeed in producing incapacitating anxiety.

**3.** Learn to accept the fact that apart from the opinions of a few significant others, what people say or think about your performance is largely irrelevant.
**4.** People who have a habit of making negative evaluations of others are not worth your trouble.

### *B. Corrective Behavior*

**1.** Note the number of times each day that you place your self-esteem on the line by thinking how well you are doing, how you may or may not be living up to a standard, and what others will think of how you perform.
**2.** When you find yourself defeating your own purposes by striving so hard to perform well that you only generate high levels of anxiety, switch off the "spectator role" by concentrating on what you are doing rather than on how well you are doing it. For example, many people with sexual inadequacies discover that they respond most gratifyingly when they focus upon giving and receiving *sensual* pleasure instead of asking themselves "How well am I doing?" or "What does he (she) think of me?"
**3.** If there is something you want to do but avoid because of "performance anxiety" (fear of failure, or concern about disapproval) choose a related task that you find relatively simple, and gradually work toward the goal you fear. For instance, in the case of a married man who avoided his wife because of "poor sexual performance," his first "task" was to kiss and caress her, while continuing to avoid any sexual contact. Thereafter the following plan proved effective: (*a*) Husband and wife engaged in prolonged kissing, hugging, and

caressing all parts of one another's bodies except genitals; (*b*) After Step (*a*) had been comfortably completed on two or three separate occasions over a week's period of time, the couple, still refraining from sexual intercourse, took turns in caressing and massaging each other, *including some genital touching;* (*c*) When Step (*b*) had been practiced on a few separate occasions, the ban on intercourse was lifted when both partners were aroused. Of course, the details will differ from case to case, but the general principle remains the same. It is also important to note that this is not simply a mechanical exercise, and the partners are requested to share their ongoing feelings during each step of the program.

## MISTAKE #19: Part 1: YOU CAN BELIEVE MOST OF WHAT YOU HEAR

## Part 2: YOUR OWN PECULIAR THOUGHTS ARE TO BE TAKEN VERY SERIOUSLY

A forty-seven-year-old man became extremely anxious after consulting an astrologist who told him that he would be dead within a year.

A young woman was experiencing anxiety. She tended to be somewhat withdrawn but was working and functioning pretty well until she went to a therapist who told her that she was schizophrenic. She developed a severe panic with suicidal thoughts and was hospitalized.

A young heterosexual man was invited to have a homosexual involvement and began wondering what it would be like. That night he had a dream about a homosexual experience. He decided that it meant that he was basically homosexual and came for therapy in a very depressed state.

*They believed:*

1. Other people's views are more correct than your own.
2. Those in authority—political leaders, heads of big businesses, teachers, clergy, doctors, parents,

therapists—necessarily know what they are talking about. "You're the doctor, you must know" or "Who am I to argue with the expert." "If a genius like Freud believed something, who are you to question it!"

3. Someone who expresses an opinion confidently is probably right.
4. What other people think or say about you is very important. If someone criticizes you, it is upsetting. Conversely, you should feel elated when someone praises you.
5. If you have a peculiar thought, it means you're crazy.

DO *YOU* BELIEVE ANY OF THIS?

## HOW TO CHANGE

### *A. Rethinking*

**1.** Other people (including the greatest authorities in the world) may be right BUT THEY MAY ALSO BE WRONG.
**2.** No one can hurt you with words. No one has the power to upset you. You are the only one who does that by the way YOU CHOOSE to react to what people say. Think about the following example: If someone said to you: "Your mother is a whore and your father is a pimp," how would you react? If you would get very angry, upset or violent, you are *giving* other people too much credence and a great deal of control over you.
**3.** If something does not jibe with your own experience, you have every right to question and challenge it, irre-

spective of who said it. Any statement is best examined in the light of evidence and data.

4. Thoughts are just thoughts and dreams are just dreams. Furthermore, there is an enormous difference between thoughts and actions. Even in our advanced civilized sophisticated culture, we are still riddled with myths and superstitions that inhibit our free expression and thwart our growth and happiness.

### *B. Corrective Behavior*

1. Catch yourself each time you *allow* someone else to upset you. Mark it down in your notebook.

2. Record in your book each time you accept someone's putting you down ("You're stupid, ugly, disturbed, not fit for college") THIS DOES NOT MEAN THAT YOU WOULDN'T LISTEN IF SOMEONE WERE GIVING YOU VALUABLE ADVICE OR CRITICISM. IT IS VERY USEFUL AND NECESSARY TO GET OTHER PEOPLE'S OPINIONS BUT YOU ARE THE ONE WHO DECIDES WHETHER THEY ARE USEFUL, RATHER THAN SIMPLY SAYING "THEY MUST KNOW, THEY MUST BE RIGHT."

3. Whenever another person expresses a strong opinion, practice saying to yourself "Does this person know what he is talking about? Does what he is saying really make sense? Is there any proof or is it simply an opinion?" Ask this NO MATTER WHO THE OTHER PERSON IS!!

4. When you get upset over a thought, feeling, or dream, practice saying to yourself "It's only a thought (feeling or dream)." Or "what a weird (silly, crazy) thought." To think crazy THOUGHTS is part of being alive. If you find yourself taking your weird thoughts seriously,

write down some of the weirder notions in your notebook (e.g., "screwing my father," "killing Aunt Matilda," "screaming in public," "drinking blood," "fondling the genitals of a two-year-old," etc.) Practice saying "So what! It's only a thought. The thought is not the deed."

## MISTAKE #20: THERAPY CAN'T HURT YOU

**A young woman sought therapy because she was unable to achieve orgasm during intercourse. She was able to have a climax with manual stimulation, but both she and her husband regarded this as abnormal. They consulted a therapist who confirmed their opinion and recommended intensive treatment for the young woman. She visited the therapist several times a week for over a year. He delved into her childhood and interpreted her dreams. She became more and more convinced that she was inadequate and sexually immature. A deep depression developed, at which time she changed therapists. Her new therapist insisted that there was nothing abnormal or immature about her sexual practices. She and her husband were then seen together for several re-educative sessions. Initially they were resistant to the notion that women who require manual stimulation are neither sexually nor emotionally immature. However, they began reading informed books and articles on the subject and developed an enlightened and satisfying sexual relationship.**

In this section we wish to emphasize that research has clearly indicated that some people are hurt (and many are not helped) by receiving the incorrect kind of therapy by the wrong types of therapists for them. The more recent technical literature deals with what is termed "therapist-caused deterioration."

Since many people will seek the assistance of a trained professional to facilitate problem-solving, we think it would be useful to share our thoughts about the qualities to look for in a therapist. Most people really have no sound basis on which to choose. Someone is recommended by a friend, neighbor, doctor, or colleague. Most therapists are trained in and practice a particular type of therapy, and in general you will get what that person knows, which may not necessarily be what is best for you. Yet, there are certain qualities and interactions which seem to be associated with successful outcomes. In general, one will see that what is recommended is a therapist who does not commit the more destructive neurotic "mistakes" with the people who consult him/her. It will be important for you to avoid some of the mistakes yourself in order to successfully utilize the services of a competent therapist; for example, "He is a trained professional so he must be right."

We've made up a list of 17 questions to help you select a therapist who would be right for you or to help you decide whether to continue seeing your present therapist. Responses are scored from 0 to 4 as follows: 0 equals never or not at all; 1, slightly or occasionally; 2, sometimes or moderately; 3, a great deal or most of the time; and 4, markedly or all of the time. Circle the number that best reflects your feelings and observations and then obtain the total score. Before reading the questions, note that it is important to consult someone trained by an accredited institution or school of psychology, psychiatry, social work, counseling or psychiatric nursing. If you have any doubt about the therapist's qualifications you can check with the county, state or national organization that licenses such people.

# Therapist-Selection Questionnaire

| | |
|---|---|
| *1)* I feel comfortable with the therapist (T). | 0 1 2 3 4 |
| *2)* T seems comfortable with me. | 0 1 2 3 4 |
| *3)* T is casual and informal rather than stiff and formal. | 0 1 2 3 4 |
| *4)* T does not treat me as if I am sick, defective, and about to fall apart. | 0 1 2 3 4 |
| *5)* T is flexible and open to new ideas rather than pursuing one point of view. | 0 1 2 3 4 |
| *6)* T has a good sense of humor and a pleasant disposition. | 0 1 2 3 4 |
| *7)* T is willing to tell me how s(he) feels about me. | 0 1 2 3 4 |

*8)* T admits limitations and does not pretend to know things s(he) doesn't know. 0 1 2 3 4

*9)* T is very willing to acknowledge being wrong and apologizes for making errors or for being inconsiderate, instead of justifying this kind of behavior. 0 1 2 3 4

*10)* T answers direct questions rather than simply asking me what I think. 0 1 2 3 4

*11)* T reveals things about herself or himself either spontaneously or in response to my inquiries (but not by bragging and talking incessantly and irrelevantly). 0 1 2 3 4

*12)* T encourages the feeling that I am as good as s(he) is. 0 1 2 3 4

*13)* T acts as if s(he) is my consultant rather than the manager of my life. 0 1 2 3 4

*14)* T encourages differences of opinion rather than telling me that I am resisting if I disagree with him or her. 0 1 2 3 4

*15)* T is interested in seeing people who share my life (or is at least willing to do so). This would include family, friends, lovers, work associates, or any other significant people in my environment. 0 1 2 3 4

*16)* The things that T says make sense to me. 0 1 2 3 4

*17)* In general, my contacts with the therapist lead to my feeling more hopeful and having higher self-esteem. 0 1 2 3 4

## How to Interpret the Score

We would not feel comfortable working with a therapist whom we rated below 50 points. Certainly, we would strongly advise people not to work with someone where the score fell below 40 points. Don't hesitate to see several therapists before choosing one. Also, decisions are not irrevocable. Don't feel that you have to stay with someone simply because you have started or have been with the same therapist for months or years. It is your time, money, and well-being that are at stake. If you have tried several therapists with different styles and personalities and none seems satisfactory, perhaps it is better to work with the one who has the highest score rather than using an absolute figure.

# Five Brief Histories You Might Find Helpful

We've written up five brief histories to illustrate some of the points made earlier. These cases will also underscore the continuity between self-help and professional therapy. We have chosen cases and instances where people responded rapidly and dramatically to our interventions. This is not intended to imply that everyone will overcome emotional problems so readily. The expenditure of time and effort will obviously vary from person to person. However, in order to acquire an optimistic view of your own potential for change, it may be helpful to realize how several people found small shifts in their thinking and behavior sufficient to produce major emotional and interpersonal changes.

## Case No. 1: Depression

A sixty-year-old woman complained that she had been feeling progressively more depressed since the sudden death of her husband eighteen months earlier. "I have nothing to look forward to," she explained, "and I often wish I were dead myself."

Her appetite was good, she slept soundly, but awoke around 7:00 A.M. feeling tired and heavy-hearted. As the day wore on, she became more weary and depressed, often to the point of exhaustion. She first consulted her internist who examined her medically and sent her for blood tests. "When the tests came back, he said I was fine and recommended that I see a psychiatrist."

She consulted a psychiatrist who put her on Elavil (an anti-depressant drug) and who saw her once a week in supportive therapy (he would listen to her problems and give her due sympathy). She continued feeling depressed and dropped out of treatment. She then consulted us at the advice of her nephew, a student who was familiar with our work.

During the initial interview it was obvious that this woman engaged in so few rewarding activities in her daily life that anyone leading her existence would probably become depressed. We explained to her that unless she deliberately found several pleasurable pursuits each and every day, she would probably continue to feel miserable and depressed. She countered with the rationalization that there were few pleasurable activities available to an old woman all on her own.

A brief inquiry revealed that she used to enjoy playing bridge, organizing church bazaars, doing crossword puzzles, being with animals, canning and making preserves, going to the zoo, working in the garden, and visiting museums. In the past eighteen months, she had pursued hardly any of the foregoing activities.

We advised her to take the initiative in calling friends and acquaintances with whom she could play bridge, visit museums, etc., and to become involved in *doing things* even if she felt tired and unhappy. "Call up a vet and volunteer your services free of charge. Ask around and see if someone would like you to make preserves for them . . . Come back in two weeks and tell me all the things you have done."

At the next interview she said that she had done three things that were new to her. "I went fishing for the first time in my life! I also had my first sauna bath, and I went to a lecture on how to care for houseplants."

"And how have you been feeling?"

"I wouldn't say all that different, and everything is such an effort."

"Well, would you make specific notes of all the things you do for the next two weeks and let me read them? And will you go out of your way to do as many things as possible even though you don't feel up to it?"

Two weeks later her notebook showed that she had carried out her assignment fairly well. She averaged three activities per day over the fourteen-day period. She reported feeling slightly less depressed.

Further discussion showed that her basic mistakes were: Mistake #4—You are a victim of circumstances ("I am depressed because my husband died." "Life has become meaningless."); Mistake #8—Make sure that you please other people and that they like and approve of you ("If I am too happy other people will say that I didn't really love my husband, and they will think less of me."); Mistake #10—You must earn happiness ("What have I ever done to deserve happiness?") She also tended to blame herself for not having taken care of her husband sufficiently well. The rethinking and corrective behavioral exercises for these mistakes were incorporated into her therapy.

At her next session she reported a breakthrough. "Last Tuesday I thought I might try taking up photography because there was a lecture near my apartment. I went to the lecture, was very bored, but met an old friend who suggested that we go to the courthouse and sit in the gallery. A man was on trial for robbery. I sat there quite fascinated and went back each day. Next week they are trying a woman who embezzled money from an insurance company . . . I have also agreed to organize a bazaar for our hospital."

A month later she reported that she had also become active in a political rally, had found a part-time job as a dentist's receptionist, had taken up embroidery, was looking forward to a visit from her daughter and grandchildren, and that she was about to embark on a course for restoring antiques. She no longer felt depressed, and whenever she felt tired, she had good reason to be fatigued. Six months later she called to say that she was feeling fine.

## Case No. 2: Anxiety Attacks

A forty-three-year-old woman whose husband had just initiated a separation came for therapy because she was markedly anxious, had frequent panic attacks, and was having difficulty sleeping and concentrating. Her husband, who had already consulted a lawyer, had moved out of their apartment. The couple had two children, a boy of eighteen and a girl of sixteen. The husband had emptied the contents of their safe-deposit box and had canceled all of her charge privileges. He was the family breadwinner and she had assumed the bulk of the household duties. She felt crushed by the rejection and wished for a reconciliation.

It was evident almost immediately that she was in trouble, not so much because of what her husband had done, but because she was committing several basic errors, most notably "You Are a Victim of Circumstances" (Mistake #4) and "Accept Other People's Opinions of You" (related to Mistake #19, Part 1). Significantly, she was much less assertive than she might have been, not only with her husband, but with her friends, her brother and sister, parents, and virtually everyone with whom she came in contact. She did not accept the idea that she was worthwhile and that she had a right to act in her own interests and to be happy. She was extremely reluctant to confront or oppose her husband. The following dialogue ensued during her second session:

T: What have you done about contacting a lawyer?

P: Nothing yet.

T: What's your plan?

P: Well, I don't know anybody.

T: What are you going to do to find out?

P: I don't know. How can I find out?

T: Suppose your children had been kidnapped and you would never see them alive again unless you had a good matrimonial lawyer by tomorrow. What would you do?

P: I guess I would call my friend Jill who just went through a divorce and seemed to have a pretty good lawyer.

T: When will you call her?

P: I guess maybe the beginning of the week.

T: "I guess" and "maybe" don't mean anything. What is your plan?

P: I will try to call this afternoon.

T: Trying doesn't mean anything either. *Doing* is what counts.

P: This afternoon, as soon as I get home.

She was upset not so much by what her husband had done, as by her interpretation of his actions. Instead of saying to herself, "It's too bad that he did that; I would have preferred that he work things out with me, but he has a right to do what's best for him; he is a free human being," etc., she felt "He did a terrible thing to me. He hurt me. He upset me. What he did was immoral. I am alone. I won't be able to find someone else. I'm pretty worthless. Who would want me? I guess I'm not good enough for him. I feel guilty for not measuring up." These latter notions were systematically challenged by the therapist. The events were certainly unpleasant and disruptive, but in fact, she could live without her husband and could find happiness elsewhere.

Her husband was threatening to cut her off without a cent and sue her for custody of the children. In the therapist's office, she was asked to practice a variety of assertive responses, for example, "Don't threaten me. I have a lawyer and the two lawyers can discuss it. Please talk to me in a quieter tone of voice. The children have a legal right for support. I have also worked (in the home) for twenty years." She also rehearsed asking for a reconciliation.

By the next session she had met with a lawyer and was feeling a little better. She no longer felt as if everything was overwhelming, and she was beginning to take steps to control her own life. She enthusiastically mentioned how assertive she had been with several people. She was well on the way to arranging her own life rather than feeling like a victim. By the third session, her anxiety attacks had stopped completely.

## Case No. 3: Marital Discord

Bill and Joan were considering divorce. Five years of marriage had brought them mixed pleasures and some very good moments, but the past year had been more negative than positive. According to Bill, their problems amounted to "a lack of communication." He also complained that their sex life was "mediocre."

We pointed out to the couple that general terms such as "poor communication" had to be translated into specific behaviors in order for change to become possible. As we discussed matters with the couple, one clear communication problem became evident. Joan very often used absolute terms such as "always" and "never." *This is a serious mistake!* She would say: "You *always* criticize my cooking." "You *never* say you're sorry." Invariably Bill would then cite examples of times and places where he had in fact complimented Joan's cooking, helped around the house, been early for an appointment, and expressed his personal regrets. In this way, they became sidetracked and argued incessantly over irrelevant details and thus suffered "a lack of communication." The first therapeutic objective was to eliminate Joan's use of absolutes.

At the same time, however, it became obvious that Bill frequently broke promises to which he had previously agreed. Bill had the habit of "forgetting" his promises and good intentions. This habit also led to unpleasant quarrels. Thus, if we could train Joan to avoid absolute words, and if we could teach Bill to keep his word, significant and constructive changes were likely to accrue.

Joan was asked to make a note each time she caught herself saying "always," or "never," and to change it to "usually," or "often," or "seldom." Furthermore, if Bill caught her saying "always," or "never," more than twice in one week, this would entitle him to have breakfast served in bed on Sunday.

Bill was advised to write down each and every promise he made. "I'll be home before six." "I'll help with the laundry tomorrow night." "I'll drive your mother to the station." If Bill failed to keep any of his promises, Joan would be served breakfast in bed on Sunday.

If Bill broke no promises and if Joan made no absolutistic comments, they would take turns serving each other breakfast in bed on Sundays as a mutual reward. They were advised to write down whose turn it would be to serve the breakfast each week.

Joan and Bill practiced these recommendations for a month on their own. We then met again to evaluate their progress. These simple but significant suggestions had brought about a profound change for the better. "I would say that in the past few weeks Joan and I have recaptured the closeness we had in the first years of our marriage." Joan agreed with Bill and added that since she felt so much closer to Bill emotionally, she was now very responsive sexually. Bill said that their sex was no longer "mediocre."

We do not wish to imply that "marriage therapy" is generally this simple or straightforward. Often, we are consulted by couples whose need to sabotage each other's gains seems to transcend their desire to save their marriages. The point of this case study is to show how it is indeed possible to effect important changes rapidly and logically with couples who are willing to carry out assignments and who cooperate with the therapeutic objectives. Quite often one can point to a few crucial mistakes and bring about widespread and positive changes by eliminating these specific errors.

## Case No. 4: Compulsions

A young man of twenty-three was a compulsive checker. He would drive himself half crazy by checking and rechecking most things five or more times. "Did I switch off the lights? Did I turn off the stove? Did I leave the car in Park? Did I remember to bring my wallet?" If he simply had reassured himself by checking such items once in a while, there would be no problem. He would be considered a cautious and conscientious individual. But the young man would go over these questions again and again. On one occasion, during a concert, he left the hall seven times to see if he had switched off the lights of his car. He explained that he would begin to feel an increasing degree of anxiety when these bothersome thoughts occurred to him and that he felt compelled to check them out.

It was very obvious that he committed Mistake #11 in most areas of his life. He tried to avoid taking risks of any kind whatsoever. It was clear that his life was so narrow and confined that he felt frustrated and angry most of the time. He worked as a junior electrician, even though his training and skills were adequate for a much higher paid position. He had no dates and lived a most drab existence.

It seemed apparent that if we could encourage him to start taking risks, his life would change for the better. But he proved to be extremely resistant to change. He saw many types of imagined dangers lurking behind every corner. He came to one session feeling suicidal. "It's no use. I might as well kill myself." The therapist responded as follows:

T: Why not kill yourself with your compulsions?
P: I don't understand.
T: Stop all your checking. Then, according to your formulation, you will be in great danger, maybe you will even die as a result.

P: That would be a slow death. I want to die quickly.

T: Well, why not have a pre-suicide week. Do everything you have never done before. Stop checking things. Ask women out on dates. Ask your employer for a raise. Go to dances. Invite friends out for dinner. Fly down to Florida for the weekend. I mean take risks and go really crazy. After that week, you can kill yourself.

It took more than the foregoing dialogue to convince him to try out a week of (for him) enormous risk taking before deciding whether or not to kill himself. But finally he agreed to take at least ten risks that week and to report back at the end of seven days. As most people might have predicted, he was no longer suicidal at the end of the week but, on the contrary, found that he was capable of overcoming his problems. A fair amount of additional work was required, but the point of this case is to demonstrate how, by overcoming one important problem area, a vital step was taken that finally led to many positive gains.

## Case No. 5: Chronic Unhappiness

Mrs. R., a fifty-two-year-old elementary school teacher complained of chronic unhappiness, tension headaches, anxiety, and depression. A discussion revealed that she had made almost every mistake in this book. The four most damaging mistakes in her case were #7, #11, #13, and #16. Thus, she seldom expressed her own needs and desires but deferred to others. She went out of her way to "play it safe," and tended to "let sleeping dogs lie" instead of asserting her rights. She regarded herself as inferior to most other people. In addition, she was also inclined to go out of her way to please other people (Mistake #8).

The various points under Rethinking and Corrective Behavior were systematically covered. While working with Mrs. R., it seemed that her *unassertiveness* was probably at the root of many of these problem areas. Like too many women in our culture, she had been raised to regard herself as a second-class citizen. She felt that "femininity" and passivity were intimately related. It was simply not "ladylike" for a woman to assert her rights.

These views were discussed in detail and challenged by the therapist. Small but significant aspects of her inhibited responses were picked up in therapy and directly altered. For example, when calling the therapist on the phone she would say, "Doctor, this is Sandy." She was "Sandy" to many people whom she called Mr., Mrs., Doctor, etc. She had an appointment coming up with her gynecologist (male) who routinely addressed her by her first name and seemed to treat her like a child.

T: Will you ask him to call you Mrs. R.? Or perhaps you can stop calling him Dr. Harris and call him Bill.

P: No. I would prefer him to call me Mrs. R.

T: Well, let's role-play it. I'll play the gynecologist. "Hello Sandy, this is Dr. Harris."

P: (pause) I can't do it.

T: You can. You mean it is hard for you. Let's start again. "Hello Sandy, this is Dr. Harris."

P: Dr. Harris, thank you for returning my call. Before we discuss my tests, I would just like to ask you if you would call me Mrs. R. instead of Sandy. I would feel more comfortable about it.

At the next session, she reported having made her assertive statement, not only to the gynecologist, but to his nurse as well. While she was pleased, she also felt guilty because she was sure that they wouldn't like her.

She felt intimidated by most people. Particular difficulty was experienced with her principal, a woman of great bitterness who was often hypercritical and insulting to the teachers. Mrs. R. was asked to recite the following statements aloud in the office, to practice them at home, and to say them a few times a day to herself at school.

1. THERE ARE NO BOSSES, ONLY EMPLOYERS.
2. I KNOW THAT I AM DOING A SATISFACTORY JOB.
3. SHE PICKS ON MOST PEOPLE, NOT JUST ME.
4. THERE IS VERY LITTLE SHE CAN DO TO HURT ME. I REALLY CANNOT BE FIRED BECAUSE I AM COMPETENT AND THERE IS A UNION.
5. IT IS TOO BAD THAT SHE IS SO UNHAPPY, BUT I WILL NO LONGER ALLOW MYSELF TO BE UPSET BY HER CRITICISM.

She was also asked to record in her notebook every unassertive episode and write out a more assertive reply that she could have made.

Role playing was done in the office with the therapist playing the part of the principal and then playing the part of Mrs. R. to show her what an assertive response would be like. The end result was that the next time the principal attacked Mrs. R., she responded as follows: "I am a human being and have feelings. Please don't raise your voice to me. If there is something specific about my work that you would like me to change, please let me know and I will do my best."

Frequent role playing during the next few sessions as well as practice by Mrs. R. between sessions led very quickly to higher self-esteem. What also proved very effective was a systematic program to increase the amount of fun in her life. Within two months most of the people who knew her were remarking about the very positive changes in her.

# A Note About Medication

We feel that the self-help techniques described in this book have widespread applicability, but there are times when the services of a professional are warranted. One such occasion is in the prescription of medication. For some individuals specific medications are vital. People with certain types of depression, with mood swings from high to low for no apparent reason, with severe anxiety, and especially persons who are prone to repeated breakdowns in which very irrational thoughts and feelings seem to be racing out of control, benefit greatly from the proper use of psychiatric drugs *in addition* to the retraining techniques we have described. Medication is no substitute for learning new thinking and behavior, though many will feel remarkably better with the right drug. Make sure that you are assertive in telling the physician whether a particular drug is helpful or not. Be sure to know the name of the drug, the dose prescribed, possible side-effects, and the reason it is being recommended. Unfortunately many of the people who could benefit from medication are not aware of its importance or do not want to take it. They feel that medication is a crutch and they want to be "independent" and do it on their own. This is recognizable as related to Mistake #12 about dependence and independence. It is no more of a crutch to take medication for certain psychological malfunctioning than it is to wear glasses when you have difficulty seeing or to take allergy pills when you are suffering miserably from hay fever. We caution you not to make the opposite error of popping pills indiscriminately as if they were answers to problems. Some people don't like taking medication because they see it as giving up control. Quite the contrary, the availability of medication gives the sufferer the power to control whatever chemical factors may be contributing to his difficulty. It is a wise person, indeed, who knows how to use the resources of the environment to better himself and promote his well-being and happiness.

# Let's Sum It Up

Over the years there has been considerable change in the fields of psychology and psychiatry. We believe wholeheartedly in the growing tendency to make therapy—problem solving—less mysterious, less complicated, and less disease-oriented. When you are dealing with a psychological or emotional difficulty, we suggest you take the following approach: (1) Define the problem. (2) Accept the idea that for the most part you learned how to think, feel, and act this way and *therefore you can unlearn it.* (3) Devise a way of measuring the problem to see how often it occurs or to what degree it occurs. For example, you would check for the frequency of a disturbing thought, the amount you are overweight. (4) Devise a way of lessening the frequency or the severity, while also increasing those positive and adaptive elements that will enhance your happiness. This latter step requires imagination and practice, and in fact you may feel at this point you would like a consultation with a trained person who is more accustomed to thinking this way. (5) Admit to yourself that if you continue to feel, act and think a certain way—the way that gives you problems—you are choosing to be that way when you could in fact find out how to change and make the special effort to change.

It's up to you! If you do not get results, it may mean that you did not work hard enough at it, or you are getting more advantages from staying the way you are, or that you and we—your therapists—were not sufficiently imaginative. *It does not mean that you are hopeless!*

We can't say this often enough: the major function of therapy is educational. To have therapy sessions or to read self-help books without practicing and without doing homework assignments is like attending lectures at school without reading or studying. It is like taking piano lessons without practicing. You may get something out of it but only a fraction of what you might otherwise have derived. Keeping a notebook, recording observations about your own thinking and behavior, and practicing new thinking and behavior are the best ways of *changing.* It is not expected that you will need to apply every example from each mistake. Work thoroughly in those areas that are most applicable to you.

For those of you who may wish to consult a therapist, we would like to remind you that we see therapy as a way to solve your problems and as a path to change. The purpose of therapy is not just to talk about your problems. We believe the therapist is someone who simply shares his/her experience. She/he is a consultant who is paid to show people certain alternatives and techniques that they might not have been aware of. It is not much different from consulting a specialist in other fields. After all, if you are trying to learn French on your own and are having difficulty, you would probably decide to take French lessons from an expert.

We want to stress at all times the importance of "self-management"—the idea that you are master of your own destiny and make your own decisions in life. You may be shown more efficient ways of doing things, but it is up to you to accept or reject the suggestions that are given. With this in mind it would be useful for you to think of other "mistakes" that you may be making, and, along the lines we have outlined, design your own prescriptions. After all, we have outlined what we think are the twenty *most common* mistakes. But there are many variations. Write down the false assumptions, and devise ways of changing fallacious thinking and faulty behaviors. Some examples of other common mistakes might be: (1) If you are different, there is something wrong with you. (2) Try to be loved and respected by everybody. (3) You can't escape your past. (4) People should be condemned for their misdeeds. There will be many others.

The solutions and prescriptions that we mention here are not new. Millions of people have been doing this kind of thing intuitively over the millennia. What we've tried to do for you is organize the material in a simple, systematic, and succinct fashion. The hope is that rather than serve as the ultimate answer to your problems, it will provide an orientation that will help you change your life in a short period of time. We earnestly believe it will and that you will gain from it. *Again,* there are very few free rides in life and effort is required to bring about change. But it has been our experience that many people who have considered themselves "disturbed," "sick," or "hopeless" for years have responded quickly to the approaches outlined in this book.

We urge you to ask yourself how important it is for you to change the things that are bothering you. Ask yourself what you would be willing to give up to bring about the changes you say you want. If you would be willing to give up a great deal, then ask yourself if you would invest half an hour a day for a few weeks or months. The results will surprise you.

At this point we would be tempted to say "Good luck" but, as you can see, luck has almost nothing to do with this enterprise. Remember: *I can if I want to.*

## *About the Authors*

Arnold Lazarus is Professor of Psychology and heads the clinical Doctor of Psychology program, Graduate School of Applied and Professional Psychology of Rutgers University. He was educated in Johannesburg, South Africa, and taught at Stanford University, Temple University Medical School, and Yale University before going to Rutgers. He has published over one hundred scientific articles on psychology.

Allen Fay is a psychiatrist in full-time private practice in New York City. He attended New York Medical College, was trained in psychiatry at Mount Sinai Hospital, and teaches behavior therapy at Mount Sinai School of Medicine of CUNY.